Sexual Revolution 2.0: Reconfiguring Norms in the Age of Digital Intimacy

Contents

Book Introduction

In the late 20th century, the world experienced a sexual revolution that forever

altered the ways we talk about, think about, and engage in sexual activities and relationships. That period shattered traditional norms and introduced the mainstream to the concept that sexuality could be openly discussed, taught, and celebrated. It was a monumental cultural shift that set the stage for the various ways we understand human sexuality today. But we are on the brink of another monumental shift—welcome to Sexual Revolution 2.0.

This book, "Sexual Revolution 2.0: Reconfiguring Norms in the Age of Digital Intimacy," aims to offer an authoritative account of how technology, social change, and evolving norms are heralding a new phase in the sexual revolution. One that's taking place not in secretive underground clubs or isolated academic settings but within the highly accessible landscape of the Internet, emerging technologies, and social media platforms.

To say we live in interesting times is a monumental understatement. The second decade of the 21st century has brought forth an explosion of dialogue around sexuality, and with it, dramatic changes in attitudes and behaviors. The global conversation around issues such as consent, gender identity, and sexual orientation is richer and more nuanced than ever before. Technology has both complicated these conversations and provided new solutions. Digital platforms have given rise to new forms of relationships, from online dating to long-distance interactive sexual experiences. The industry of "sextech" is burgeoning, challenging taboos and reshaping the very mechanics of sexual pleasure.

In the following chapters, you will be introduced to various facets of this new revolution. We delve into the new vocabulary of desire, elaborating on how emerging terms are capturing complex sexual and emotional orientations. We explore consent culture in the digital era, an environment rife with both opportunities and pitfalls. We also consider the roles that emerging technologies are playing in reshaping the boundaries of fantasy and reality. Alongside this, we will tackle the evolving landscape of gender fluidity, LGBTQ+ perspectives, and new sexual identities that are gaining visibility.

Additionally, we touch on the reimagining of pornography, the rewriting of sex education, and the changing dynamics of relationships, whether they be monogamous or polyamorous. No conversation would be complete without addressing sex work in the modern era, as well as the laws and policies that are struggling to keep up with rapid changes in sexual mores. Lastly, the future of sexual health and the ethical and philosophical considerations that come with these changes are discussed in depth.

Sexuality, in all its shades and complexities, is an integral part of human existence. It's high time that we approach it with the openness, understanding, and analytical rigor it deserves. Whether you're an academic, a practitioner, or simply someone keen to understand the future of sexuality, this book will provide you with a comprehensive guide to navigating the intricacies of Sexual Revolution 2.0. Prepare to challenge your preconceptions, open your mind to new realities, and perhaps even redefine your own sexual self-concept.

Welcome to the future. Welcome to Sexual Revolution 2.0.

Chapter 1: Introduction: Beyond the First Wave

In the 1960s and 70s, the world experienced a seismic shift in sexual attitudes and behaviors that came to be known as the Sexual Revolution. This period saw the widespread adoption of contraceptive methods, a loosening of social mores, and the democratization of sexual information. Gone were the rigid frameworks that boxed sexuality into narrow definitions; suddenly, it became conceivable to talk about, study, and practice a broader array of sexual behaviors and identities. However, as radical as those times were, they were merely the prelude to something even more profound. We find ourselves now in the midst of Sexual Revolution 2.0, a continuation and elaboration of that initial wave but with complexities that could scarcely have been imagined in the days of flower power and free love.

The First Wave: Setting the Stage

To fully appreciate the scope of the current revolution, it's essential to revisit its predecessor briefly. The original sexual revolution was fueled by a myriad of socio-political factors, most notably the advent of the contraceptive pill, which provided an unprecedented level of control over reproductive choices. Social change was in the air, propelled by the civil rights movement, second-wave feminism, and the anti-war sentiment. Sexuality became an arena for challenging the status quo, whether that meant promoting women's sexual agency, endorsing LGBTQ+ rights, or simply divorcing the act of sex from its procreative function. This era of liberation laid the groundwork for many of the freedoms we enjoy today, but it was not without its limitations.

The Catalysts of Change: Technology and Information

While the first wave was facilitated by medical technology and changes in law, Sexual Revolution 2.0 is shaped by digital technology and an explosion of information. The Internet, perhaps the most influential tool of our age, has democratized sexual knowledge to an extent unimaginable just a few decades ago. No longer are we reliant on whispered rumors, arcane medical texts, or uncomfortable parent-child talks. The digital age has granted us access to a treasure trove of information—much of it user-generated, hence sidestepping institutional bias—that addresses every conceivable facet of human sexuality.

The New Social Paradigms

The first wave was primarily a Western phenomenon, limited by geography and cultural reach. However, Sexual Revolution 2.0 is inherently global, thanks to the connective power of social media and the Internet. The globalization of sexual mores is an astonishing development, causing both friction and integration between contrasting cultural attitudes toward sex. And it's not just about the dissemination of Western ideologies; there's a reciprocal exchange of ideas that's enriching our understanding of what sexual freedom can mean.

Sexuality in the Modern World

The impact of technology on sexuality is not merely informational but also practical. Virtual spaces offer new realms for sexual expression and exploration, from the simple swipe right to the intricate possibilities of virtual reality sex. Yet, these developments also raise questions about the commodification of intimacy, the ethics of online interaction, and the potential for exploitation or abuse.

Breaking the Taboos: A New Generation

While the first sexual revolution had its radicals and pioneers, the new generation, armed with information and emboldened by a sense of social justice, is shattering taboos with even greater vigor. They are questioning normative structures at a fundamental level, examining issues like consent, gender identity, and sexual orientation with a nuanced lens that's both analytical and empathetic.

In the chapters that follow, we will delve deeper into these topics, examining the many facets of Sexual Revolution 2.0. We will look at how this ongoing transformation is affecting our language, our relationships, our laws, and even our own understanding of what it means to be a sexual being. The age of Sexual

Revolution 2.0 is upon us, and it's more intricate, more inclusive, and more revolutionary than anything we've experienced before.

With this foundational understanding, prepare to venture further into the landscape of modern sexuality as we take this intellectual and cultural journey together. This book aims to be your guide, providing you with the necessary tools to navigate, understand, and partake in Sexual Revolution 2.0.

Chapter 2: The New Vocabulary of Desire

The way we talk about anything shapes how we think about it. Language is not merely a tool for communication but also a framework for understanding the world. This is especially true when it comes to human sexuality, a domain so intricate, so subjective, and so bound up with identity that the words we use to describe it can profoundly influence both personal and societal attitudes. In the age of Sexual Revolution 2.0, language is evolving at an accelerated rate, creating a new vocabulary of desire that captures the complexity and diversity of modern sexual experiences.

The Inadequacy of Traditional Language

Traditional language around sexuality has often been binary, limiting, and steeped in societal norms that reflect restrictive notions of gender, orientation, and behavior. The terms 'male' and 'female,' 'gay' and 'straight,' 'vanilla' and 'kinky,' while still in use, are increasingly seen as inadequate for capturing the full spectrum of human sexuality. As we evolve in our understanding, so must our language.

Inclusivity and Specificity

One of the most striking features of the new vocabulary is its emphasis on inclusivity. Words like 'cisgender,' 'non-binary,' 'pansexual,' and 'asexual' reflect a desire to acknowledge a broader range of identities and orientations than traditional language permits. These terms offer people the specificity they need to describe their experiences accurately, which in turn fosters greater understanding and acceptance.

The Role of Internet Communities

The rise of online spaces dedicated to specific sexual interests, identities, or orientations has spurred much of this linguistic innovation. Internet communities act as incubators for new terminology, allowing individuals to articulate their experiences and preferences with a level of nuance hitherto unimaginable. From Reddit forums to TikTok videos, these platforms are both creating and disseminating the new vocabulary of desire at an unprecedented rate.

Sex-Positive Language

Sex-positivity, an attitude towards human sexuality that regards all consensual sexual activities as fundamentally healthy and pleasurable, has significantly influenced this evolving lexicon. Terms like 'ethical non-monogamy,' 'consent culture,' and 'body positivity' reinforce the idea that sexuality should be approached with openness, mutual respect, and an absence of judgment.

The Words for New Technologies

As technological innovations continue to impact sexual experiences, our language has adapted to incorporate these developments. Terms like 'teledildonics,' which refers to electronic sex toys that can be controlled remotely, or 'virtual intimacy,' indicating a type of closeness achieved through digital means, showcase how language evolves to encapsulate modern phenomena.

Intersectionality in Language

Language around sexuality is increasingly incorporating an understanding of intersectionality, recognizing that sexual identity doesn't exist in a vacuum but is interwoven with other social categorizations such as race, class, and disability. This gives rise to terms like 'queer POC' (People of Color), 'disabled sexuality,' or 'working-class LGBTQ,' which attempt to capture the complexity of lived experiences.

The Backlash and the Future

While the new vocabulary of desire offers an inclusive, nuanced way to talk about sexuality, it's not without its critics. Some argue that the proliferation of terms can be confusing, divisive, or exclusionary in its own right. However, the ongoing conversation, even the debate, around this evolving language is a hallmark of Sexual Revolution 2.0. It's a sign that we're actively engaging with the complexity of human sexuality, challenging our preconceptions, and striving for a more inclusive future.

In the chapters to come, many of these terms will recur, serving as critical tools for exploring the multifaceted landscape of modern sexuality. They are the language of Sexual Revolution 2.0, a lexicon that allows us to speak about desire, identity, and intimacy with unprecedented accuracy and empathy.

Chapter 3: Consent Culture in the Digital Age

As we move deeper into the era of Sexual Revolution 2.0, one theme resonates strongly across various dimensions of sexual behavior and interaction: the culture of consent. Consent isn't a new concept; it has long been recognized as a cornerstone of ethical sexual behavior. However, the ways we think about, talk about, and practice consent are undergoing a revolutionary transformation, significantly shaped by the digital landscape in which many of our interactions now occur.

The Old Guard: "No Means No"

The traditional paradigm for understanding sexual consent has often been summed up in the phrase "no means no." While this slogan served as a crucial first step in highlighting the importance of explicit refusal, it is increasingly viewed as inadequate. The problem lies in its focus on refusal rather than affirmative agreement, thus putting the onus on individuals to resist unwanted advances rather than encouraging mutual, enthusiastic consent.

Affirmative Consent: "Yes Means Yes"

Today's evolving norms advocate for a model of affirmative consent, frequently encapsulated in the new slogan "yes means yes." This model demands an explicit, enthusiastic, and ongoing agreement from all parties involved. It isn't just about saying 'yes' once but about ensuring that all individuals are comfortable and on board at every stage of a sexual encounter.

The Digital Complication

Digital technologies complicate the dynamics of consent in multiple ways. On the one hand, platforms like messaging apps and social media can facilitate open discussions about consent, preferences, and boundaries before any physical encounter takes place. On the other hand, these technologies create new arenas where violations of consent can occur, such as non-consensual sharing of intimate images, also known as "revenge porn," or harassment via direct messages.

Consent in Virtual Spaces

As sexual interactions increasingly extend into virtual realms—through sexting, video calls, and even virtual reality—the parameters of consent become hazier. Does consent to a physical act automatically extend to a virtual reenactment of that act? What does it mean to violate someone's consent in a digital space? These are questions we are only beginning to explore, but they are crucial for ethical sexual behavior in the modern world.

Communication is Key

One aspect that hasn't changed is the importance of communication. The tools might be different—text messages instead of whispered conversations, emoji instead of body language—but the fundamental need for open, honest, and ongoing communication remains the same. In the digital age, clear dialogues about consent are both more possible and more necessary than ever before.

Navigating Power Dynamics

The culture of consent in the digital age also calls for a nuanced understanding of power dynamics. This entails recognizing how factors like age, social status, and even tech-savviness can influence one's ability to give or withhold consent freely. In this context, consent isn't just about individual acts but also about systemic inequalities that can bias our sexual interactions.

New Frontiers: AI and Ethics

As artificial intelligence and machine learning technologies advance, we're nearing a point where we may have to consider the ethics of consent in interactions with humanoid robots or highly advanced virtual personalities. Though they lack consciousness, their potential to mimic human-like responses could blur the boundaries of what we consider to be ethical sexual behavior.

Towards a New Normal

The notion of consent is expanding and adapting to accommodate the multifaceted ways in which we interact in the digital age. The responsibility lies with each one of us to actively engage with this evolving culture of consent, not just for our benefit but also as a collective commitment to more ethical, respectful, and empathetic sexual interactions.

As we proceed through the subsequent chapters, the underlying theme of consent will recur, intertwined with topics like technology, language, and social change. This focus on consent doesn't narrow the scope of our inquiry but rather enriches it, serving as a foundational ethic for navigating the complex landscape of Sexual Revolution 2.0.

Chapter 4: Gender Fluidity and Its Impact

The changing dynamics of sexual orientation and identity are irrevocably transforming our society, and one of the most pivotal changes lies in our increasingly nuanced understanding of gender. Gone are the days when gender was considered a binary concept, solely based on biological or anatomical distinctions. Today, the notion of gender fluidity is at the forefront of the Sexual Revolution 2.0, making significant impacts across various sectors of society, from individual self-identifications to institutional policies.

Understanding Gender Fluidity

The term 'gender fluidity' refers to the idea that gender is not fixed but can change over time and across different contexts. It shatters the long-standing binary of male/female, allowing for a spectrum of identities that can include non-binary, genderqueer, genderfluid, and more. This fluidity extends to gender expression and roles, acknowledging that how one presents oneself to the world may also be a variable factor, separate from one's biological sex or self-identified gender.

Societal Impacts: Beyond the Restroom Debate

While restroom access remains a hot-button issue, the implications of acknowledging gender fluidity extend much further. They touch upon all aspects of daily life, from the language we use and the clothes we wear to broader societal constructs like the family unit, workplace dynamics, and even legal systems. The impacts are profound, challenging ingrained norms and opening the door for more inclusive environments.

Intersectionality: Gender and Other Social Factors

The concept of gender fluidity becomes even more complex when we consider it in the context of intersectionality. The way an individual experiences their gender can be profoundly influenced by other intersecting identities such as race, class, and sexuality. Acknowledging this intersectionality enriches our understanding and fosters a more nuanced dialogue around gender issues.

The Medical Community's Role

Healthcare is another sector where the recognition of gender fluidity is having transformative effects. Medical professionals are increasingly moving away from pathologizing non-binary or fluid gender identities and toward a model of care that respects individual self-definition. This is impacting everything from mental health services to reproductive healthcare and even emergency medicine.

Gender Fluidity in Media Representation

The portrayal of gender-fluid characters in media is gradually becoming more common, but there's a long way to go in terms of accurate and diverse representation. The increasing visibility of gender-fluid individuals in mainstream media does, however, signify a broader social acceptance and sparks important conversations around gender norms.

Technology: A Double-Edged Sword

On one hand, digital platforms provide a space for gender-fluid individuals to connect, share experiences, and find community. On the other, the anonymity of the online world can also make them targets for harassment and discrimination. As technology continues to shape our interactions, it holds both the promise of unprecedented inclusivity and the peril of deepening divides.

Education and Youth

The impact of gender fluidity is perhaps most apparent among younger generations, who are growing up with a far more expansive understanding of gender than their predecessors. Schools are adapting, albeit slowly, incorporating inclusive language and policies. But the debate over topics like gender education in schools shows that societal attitudes still have a long way to go.

The Path Forward

The recognition and acceptance of gender fluidity are not merely trends or buzzwords; they are the manifestations of a deeper, more fundamental shift in understanding human diversity. This shift is both a cause and a consequence of

Sexual Revolution 2.0, contributing to a broader reevaluation of what it means to be human in today's world.

As we delve further into the nuances of modern sexuality in the chapters ahead, the topic of gender fluidity will reappear, intersecting with other themes like consent, technology, and social change. Its role is central, not peripheral, to understanding the myriad ways in which our ideas about sexuality and identity are undergoing rapid transformation.

Chapter 5: Virtual Realms: Sexuality in Digital Spaces

The digital world is no longer a separate entity from the real world; it has integrated itself into every facet of our lives, profoundly shaping how we interact, communicate, and even experience sexuality. This chapter delves into the complex relationship between digital spaces and human sexuality, examining how the internet, social media, and emerging technologies are redefining the landscape of sexual interaction and expression.

Digital Communities: The New Social Norm

Digital platforms have become the primary hubs for communities built around specific sexual orientations, fetishes, or interests. These platforms offer spaces for people to explore their sexuality in a relatively safe and anonymous environment. However, these spaces are not without their challenges, including issues of consent and harassment, which we touched upon in Chapter 3.

Dating Apps: The Swipe Revolution

The way we seek out romantic or sexual partners has been revolutionized by dating apps. No longer confined to our immediate social circles, we can now connect with people from different geographic locations and social backgrounds. But while these apps offer a world of possibilities, they also come with pitfalls such as catfishing, 'ghosting,' and the commodification of attraction.

Sexting and Virtual Intimacy

Digital spaces also enable forms of sexual expression like sexting, which, for some, offers a liberating avenue for sexual creativity. Yet, the virtual nature of these interactions often complicates the traditional understanding of consent and boundaries, reiterating the need for a robust culture of affirmative consent in the digital realm.

Teledildonics: The Future of Remote Intimacy?

With advancements in technology, particularly teledildonics, long-distance couples or even strangers can now experience a form of physical intimacy through the internet. This development pushes us to expand our definitions of physicality and presence, challenging traditional ideas of what sexual interaction can encompass.

Virtual Reality: A New Frontier

Virtual reality (VR) takes digital sexual experiences to a whole new level, offering immersive experiences that can either replicate real-life scenarios or create entirely fantastical settings. While this offers exciting possibilities, it also raises ethical concerns, particularly regarding consent and the potential for more immersive forms of pornography or sexual content that may blur the lines between reality and simulation.

Digital Kink Communities

The internet has also been a boon for communities interested in BDSM and other forms of kink, offering not only spaces for discussion and connection but also educational resources for safe and consensual practices. These communities exemplify how digital spaces can foster a more informed and ethical sexual culture.

The Dark Side: Exploitation and Abuse

However, the digital world is not without its dark corners, including spaces where non-consensual or exploitative behaviors occur, such as revenge porn, online stalking, and child exploitation. These are reminders that digital platforms are tools that can be used for both empowerment and abuse.

Surveillance and Privacy

The pervasiveness of digital technology in our sexual lives also raises questions about privacy and surveillance. Who owns the intimate data we share? What happens if it gets into the wrong hands? These are pressing concerns as we navigate the intersection of sexuality and technology.

Where Do We Go From Here?

As digital spaces continue to reshape our sexual realities, it's crucial to consider the ethical, social, and psychological implications. While these platforms offer liberating opportunities for exploration and expression, they also necessitate a renewed commitment to consent, education, and mutual respect.

In upcoming chapters, the role of digital spaces will continue to intersect with themes ranging from consent culture to gender fluidity, reinforcing how deeply integrated these virtual realms have become in the fabric of Sexual Revolution 2.0.

Chapter 6: Sextech: Beyond Taboo to Everyday Use

As we further explore the nuanced landscape of Sexual Revolution 2.0, it's impossible to ignore the role of technology specifically designed to enhance or facilitate sexual experiences—commonly known as "sextech." What was once considered taboo is increasingly becoming mainstream, as the sector evolves from the shadows into a multi-billion-dollar industry. This chapter unpacks the many dimensions of sextech, from its applications for health and education to its impact on relationships, examining how it has moved beyond the realm of taboo to find a place in everyday use.

The Many Faces of Sextech

Sextech encompasses a wide range of technologies and devices aimed at improving, enhancing, or facilitating sexual experiences. This includes everything from advanced sex toys with smart functionalities to virtual reality pornography, from apps focused on improving sexual health to platforms designed to educate people about consent and sexual wellness.

Health Applications: More than Just Pleasure

While sextech is often associated primarily with pleasure, its applications extend far beyond that. Devices and apps that help with issues like erectile dysfunction, premature ejaculation, or even fertility tracking are becoming more prevalent. These are not just gadgets but medical aids that are breaking the stigma surrounding sexual health.

Accessibility and Inclusivity

One of the most significant strides in sextech is its focus on inclusivity. Products designed for people with disabilities or those who have unique anatomical needs are becoming more common. This democratization of pleasure and sexual well-being highlights how technology can be leveraged for social good.

Sex Education: The Digital Classroom

Sextech isn't just about devices; it's also about information. Numerous platforms now offer comprehensive sexual education, targeting gaps left by inadequate or biased traditional educational systems. These resources are essential tools for fostering a culture of consent and mutual respect, themes we've emphasized in earlier chapters.

The Role in Long-Term Relationships

For couples in long-term relationships, sextech offers an array of tools to maintain or reignite intimacy. Whether it's apps that facilitate open discussion about sexual desires or smart toys that can be controlled remotely, technology is helping long-term partners explore new dimensions of their sexuality.

Ethical Concerns: Consent and Data

As with any technology, sextech comes with its set of ethical concerns. The issue of consent in the use of remotely controlled devices or the sharing of intimate data collected by smart toys remains a subject of debate. These questions emphasize the need for responsible innovation and ethical guidelines in the industry.

Regulatory Challenges

The sextech industry also faces unique regulatory hurdles, from the classification of devices as medical equipment to issues surrounding the legality of certain virtual experiences. These challenges indicate a gap in existing legal frameworks, which are struggling to catch up with the pace of technological advancement.

Consumer Dynamics: Normalizing the Conversation

As sextech becomes more mainstream, consumer attitudes are shifting. What was once purchased in secrecy is now openly discussed, reviewed, and even recommended among friends. This normalization is a critical aspect of how sextech is moving beyond taboo, as it encourages more open conversations about sexual health and pleasure.

The Future of Sextech

As technology continues to evolve, the applications for sextech will undoubtedly expand. Whether it's the integration of artificial intelligence to create more personalized experiences or the development of devices that can monitor and improve sexual health in real-time, the future is promising.

As you've likely gleaned from this and previous chapters, the advent of technology is deeply interwoven with the evolution of sexual culture in our society. From consent to gender fluidity, from virtual realms to sextech, each new development offers both unprecedented opportunities and complex challenges.

Chapter 7: Kink and Fetish: The New Normal

In a society characterized by increasing openness about sexuality, it's no surprise that kink and fetish practices, once seen as taboos or perversions, are emerging as more broadly accepted facets of human sexuality. In the context of Sexual Revolution 2.0, kink and fetish are no longer on the fringes but are becoming increasingly incorporated into mainstream dialogue and practice. This chapter delves into this fascinating subject, examining its normalization, its cultural and psychological dimensions, and its intricate relationship with technology, consent, and community.

The Changing Narrative

For a long time, kink and fetish were relegated to the hidden corners of sexual culture. However, the growth of online communities, coupled with more open discussions in media, have contributed to the destigmatization and democratization of these practices. We're now seeing kink-themed events, workshops, and even academic courses focusing on the subject.

Definition and Spectrum

It's crucial to understand what we mean when we talk about kink and fetish. While these terms are often used interchangeably, they are distinct. Kink broadly refers to unconventional sexual preferences or practices, while a fetish is a specific form of kink focused on a particular object, material, or body part. The spectrum of kinks and fetishes is incredibly diverse, ranging from BDSM (Bondage, Discipline, Sadism, Masochism) to various role-playing scenarios, and much more.

The Psychology of Kink

Recent research has begun to explore the psychological aspects of engaging in kink and fetish activities. Far from being seen as 'abnormal,' these practices can offer enhanced emotional connection, stress relief, and even personal growth. Understanding the psychological drivers behind kink also promotes a more informed and nuanced conversation around it.

Kink, Fetish, and Consent

As we have emphasized in previous chapters, the foundation of any healthy sexual interaction is consent. This principle is particularly pertinent in the realm of kink and fetish, where activities might involve power dynamics, physical restraints, or even pain. Open communication, mutual respect, and explicit consent are not just optional; they are essential.

Technology's Role

As discussed in Chapter 6, technology has also found its way into the world of kink. From smart BDSM toys that ensure safer practices to online platforms that allow for the exploration and negotiation of kinks, technology is a game-changer. It provides not only tools but also educational resources to foster a culture of informed and consensual kink practices.

The Community Aspect

Kink and fetish practices often have a strong community element. Whether it's online forums, social media groups, or physical venues like dungeons or clubs, these spaces offer support, education, and a sense of belonging. They provide venues for people to explore their interests in a safe and judgment-free environment.

Intersectionality and Inclusion

The conversation around kink and fetish is becoming increasingly intersectional, taking into account how these practices intersect with other aspects of identity such as gender, race, and sexual orientation. The need for more inclusive spaces and dialogues around kink is becoming evident, a theme that aligns with the broader goals of Sexual Revolution 2.0.

The Future: Beyond Normalization

What does the future hold for kink and fetish as they continue to be normalized? Will they be fully integrated into mainstream sexual education? Will new forms of kink emerge with technological advancements? While it's hard to predict, what's clear is that the conversation around these topics will continue to evolve, characterized by greater openness, inclusivity, and sophistication.

Kink and fetish practices, once sidelined, have found a place in the spotlight, indicative of a society that is learning not just to accept but to embrace sexual diversity in all its forms. As with other topics we've discussed, from gender fluidity to sextech, the acceptance of kink and fetish is both a cause and an effect of the evolving landscape of human sexuality.

Chapter 8: LGBTQ+ Perspectives: More Than Just Letters

As we traverse the ever-expanding landscape of Sexual Revolution 2.0, the inclusion and representation of LGBTQ+ perspectives are not just important but vital. A meaningful sexual revolution is one that elevates the experiences of all individuals across the sexual orientation and gender identity spectrum. The stories, challenges, and triumphs of LGBTQ+ individuals are not merely supplementary; they are integral to a fuller understanding of contemporary sexuality. This chapter aims to delve into various aspects of LGBTQ+ experiences, breaking them down to more than just a collection of letters.

The Historical Context

The LGBTQ+ community has a rich, albeit often painful, history marked by struggles for recognition, acceptance, and rights. Understanding this historical context is essential for grasping the significance of current advancements and challenges. It allows us to appreciate not just where we are but how far we've come.

Sexual Orientation and Gender Identity: Clarifying Terms

Though often grouped together, sexual orientation and gender identity are distinct facets of human diversity. Sexual orientation pertains to who you are attracted to, while gender identity relates to your internal sense of your own gender. Both of these can be fluid, adding layers of complexity to LGBTQ+ experiences that are critical to understand.

Coming Out and Self-Identification

One significant rite of passage for many LGBTQ+ individuals is the act of 'coming out'—publicly disclosing one's sexual orientation or gender identity. While increasingly common and often celebrated, coming out remains fraught with emotional and sometimes physical risks. Each coming out story is unique and underscores the complexity and diversity within the LGBTQ+ community.

Discrimination and Legal Battles

Despite societal progress, discrimination against LGBTQ+ individuals persists, manifesting in various forms such as housing discrimination, workplace bias, and healthcare disparities. Simultaneously, legal battles for rights such as same-sex marriage and transgender healthcare continue to be fought worldwide, highlighting that the revolution is far from complete.

Queer Spaces and Communities

Much like kink and fetish communities discussed in Chapter 7, LGBTQ+ individuals often find solace, empowerment, and camaraderie in queer spaces, both physical and online. These spaces are vital for collective activism, personal well-being, and social interaction, serving as nurturing grounds for culture and identity.

Intersectionality in the LGBTQ+ Context

LGBTQ+ individuals do not live single-issue lives. Many navigate the world at the intersection of various social categories, including race, class, and disability, which compound their experiences of privilege or oppression. This intersectionality adds another layer of complexity to LGBTQ+ perspectives.

Representation in Media and Culture

Media representation matters. Positive and accurate portrayals of LGBTQ+ characters in movies, television, and literature contribute to broader social acceptance and understanding. While there has been significant progress, much work remains to be done to ensure that such representation is diverse and inclusive.

LGBTQ+ and Technology

As touched upon in previous chapters, technology plays a significant role in the lives of LGBTQ+ individuals, from dating apps tailored to the community to online forums that provide much-needed support and advice. These platforms are double-edged swords, offering both opportunities and challenges that are unique to LGBTQ+ experiences.

Future Perspectives

The rights and recognition of LGBTQ+ individuals have come a long way, but the journey is ongoing. The rise of conservative movements, ongoing legal battles, and persistent discrimination indicate that much work lies ahead. However, the resilience and activism of the LGBTQ+ community give reason for optimism.

In sum, any exploration of contemporary sexuality would be incomplete without including LGBTQ+ perspectives. These experiences, shaped by unique challenges and triumphs, enrich our understanding of sexual diversity, highlighting that these are not just letters but vibrant, complex lives that make

Sexual Revolution 2.0 truly revolutionary.

Chapter 9: Pornography Reimagined

The topic of pornography has long been a contentious one, fraught with moral, ethical, and societal dilemmas. However, within the context of Sexual Revolution 2.0, the dialogue surrounding porn is undergoing a significant transformation. This chapter aims to dissect the ways in which pornography is being reimagined in our modern society, from its production and consumption to its influence on sexual education and relationships.

Historical Overview: From Taboo to Mainstream

A cursory look at the history of pornography reveals how its status has fluctuated between periods of prohibition and acceptance. As society advances, however, pornography has indisputably become more mainstream, accessible, and diversified, partially owing to the proliferation of the internet.

Ethical Pornography: A Growing Movement

One of the most noteworthy developments in modern pornography is the rise of "ethical porn"—content created with explicit consent, fair pay for performers, and an attention to diverse representation. This form of pornography challenges the established norms and provides an alternative that aligns more closely with the values of Sexual Revolution 2.0.

The Psychology of Consumption

The consumption of pornography is a multifaceted behavior influenced by various psychological factors, from curiosity to sexual gratification, and even emotional comfort. Contrary to stigmatized perceptions, consuming pornography does not necessarily imply deviance or dysfunction, but rather another aspect of human sexuality that deserves nuanced understanding.

Gender Perspectives in Pornography

Traditionally male-dominated, the landscape of pornography is undergoing a shift to become more inclusive of women and non-binary individuals, not just as consumers but also as producers. The gendered dynamics of pornography are changing, giving way to a more egalitarian landscape.

Pornography and Sexual Education

In an age where formal sexual education often falls short, many turn to pornography as an educational tool. While this is a controversial subject, some argue that ethical, realistic pornography can serve as a supplement to comprehensive sexual education, filling in the gaps left by traditional curricula.

The Dark Side: Exploitation and Addiction

While this chapter emphasizes the reimagining of pornography, it is crucial to acknowledge its darker aspects, such as exploitation, non-consensual sharing ("revenge porn"), and potential for addiction. These issues underline the need for regulation, education, and responsible consumption.

Technology and Pornography

As discussed in previous chapters, technology has a pervasive impact on human sexuality, and the realm of pornography is no exception. From virtual reality to interactive toys, technology is revolutionizing the ways in which porn is produced and consumed.

Legislation and Policy

Pornography often exists in a complex legal framework that varies significantly from jurisdiction to jurisdiction. The laws governing its production and consumption can be moral, practical, or a combination of both, influencing how society interacts with and controls this form of media.

The Future of Pornography

As society becomes more open in its discussions about sexuality, and as technology continues to evolve, what could the future hold for pornography? Could it become more integrated into mainstream culture, or will it always retain a veneer of taboo?

In the context of Sexual Revolution 2.0, the reimagining of pornography signifies a broader shift in attitudes toward human sexuality. As ethical considerations, technological advancements, and cultural changes intersect, they contribute to a complex but increasingly open dialogue that challenges us to rethink our preconceptions and engage with the subject matter in more thoughtful and nuanced ways.

Chapter 10: Sex Education: Rewriting the Curriculum

In the midst of Sexual Revolution 2.0, the importance of comprehensive, inclusive, and fact-based sex education cannot be overstated. For decades, traditional models of sex education have been woefully inadequate, often propagating harmful myths, gender stereotypes, and heteronormative viewpoints. This chapter aims to dissect the shortcomings of existing curricula and explore how sex education is being rewritten to better reflect the realities and complexities of modern human sexuality.

The State of Sex Education: A Critical Assessment

Though varying widely from one jurisdiction to another, sex education has often been limited to biological aspects of reproduction, excluding important topics such as consent, sexual orientation, gender identity, and emotional intelligence.

This chapter begins with a critique of the existing state of sex education, setting the stage for the discussions that follow.

The Rise of Comprehensive Sex Education

Comprehensive sex education (CSE) is gradually gaining recognition as the most effective approach to teaching young people about sexuality. Going beyond mere mechanics, CSE encompasses a broad range of topics including anatomy, contraception, sexually transmitted infections (STIs), relationships, consent, and sexual orientation, among others.

Consent: A Core Component

One glaring omission in many traditional sex education curricula is the concept of consent. With the rise of consent culture, the importance of teaching young people about mutual agreement and boundaries is increasingly being acknowledged. In this revamped curriculum, consent takes its rightful place as a core component.

Inclusion of LGBTQ+ Perspectives

As discussed in Chapter 8, LGBTQ+ perspectives are integral to a comprehensive understanding of human sexuality. An inclusive curriculum recognizes these perspectives, addressing topics like same-sex relationships, gender fluidity, and the unique challenges faced by LGBTQ+ individuals in a heteronormative society.

The Role of Technology

Technology is not just a disruptor but also an enabler, providing new avenues for sex education. From interactive online courses to apps that simulate various scenarios, technology can complement traditional teaching methods, making education more accessible and engaging.

Navigating Cultural Sensitivities

Sex education often exists at the intersection of education policy and cultural beliefs, making it a subject fraught with controversy. This section explores how to navigate these sensitivities without compromising the integrity and comprehensiveness of the curriculum.

Parental Involvement: Partnership or Pitfall?

While parental involvement in sex education can be beneficial, it can also introduce biases and gaps in information. This section delves into the delicate balance that must be struck between encouraging parental input and maintaining an evidence-based approach.

Reaching the Marginalized

Access to quality sex education is often a matter of social justice. This section highlights the need to extend comprehensive, unbiased, and factual sex education to marginalized communities, including those in low-income areas and individuals with disabilities.

Case Studies: Success Stories and Lessons Learned

Real-world examples serve as both inspiration and cautionary tales. This section features case studies that demonstrate the impact of progressive sex education policies and programs.

The Future of Sex Education

With ongoing cultural shifts and technological advancements, what does the future hold for sex education? This concluding section speculates on upcoming trends and challenges, emphasizing the need for continuous adaptation and improvement.

Sex education is not merely a subject to be glossed over in school; it is a critical component of human development and well-being. By rewriting the curriculum to better reflect the complexities of modern sexuality, society takes a significant step forward in empowering individuals to lead safer, healthier, and more fulfilling lives. It is a necessary evolution, wholly in line with the broader aspirations of Sexual Revolution 2.0.

Chapter 11: Navigating Relationships: Monogamy, Polyamory, and Beyond

Relationship structures are undergoing a reevaluation in the era of Sexual Revolution 2.0. Gone are the days when monogamy was the one-size-fits-all approach to love and intimacy. A spectrum of possibilities now exists, ranging from traditional monogamy to ethical non-monogamy, polyamory, and other alternative relationship models. This chapter aims to explore these evolving dynamics, providing a nuanced look at how modern society navigates relationships.

The Dominance of Monogamy: Historical Roots

The cultural prevalence of monogamy has deep historical and sociological roots, from religious edicts to economic incentives. Understanding the reasons behind monogamy's dominance can provide insight into why alternative relationship models have been marginalized, and how this is beginning to change.

Ethical Non-Monogamy: A Primer

Ethical non-monogamy is an umbrella term that includes various forms of relationships that are consensually non-exclusive. This section provides an overview, distinguishing it from infidelity by its cornerstone principles of consent, communication, and honesty.

Polyamory: Love Without Limits

Polyamory is a form of ethical non-monogamy that allows individuals to openly have multiple loving relationships simultaneously. This section delves into the nuances of polyamorous relationships, including their different configurations and the challenges and rewards they offer.

Beyond Gender Norms: Relationship Anarchy

Moving further along the spectrum, relationship anarchy challenges not just exclusivity but also the very hierarchies that exist in relationships. It asserts that love should not be restricted by labels or categories, emphasizing autonomy and personalized relationship structures.

The Emotional Landscape: Jealousy, Compersion, and More

Feelings of jealousy are often cited as a reason why alternative relationship models might not work. However, proponents argue that jealousy can be managed and even transformed into compersion, the feeling of joy one experiences when a loved one is happy with another person. This section examines the emotional intricacies involved in various relationship models.

The Legal Aspect: Marriage, Contracts, and Custody

As relationship structures diversify, legal systems are often slow to catch up. This section explores the implications for marriage, contractual arrangements, and child custody, highlighting areas where change is needed to accommodate non-traditional relationships.

Technology's Role in Modern Relationships

From dating apps that cater to polyamorous individuals to online communities that offer support and advice, technology plays a pivotal role in how modern relationships are formed and maintained. This section examines the advantages and pitfalls of technology in navigating complex relationship structures.

Communicating Needs: The Importance of Open Dialogue

In any relationship model, communication is key. This section emphasizes the vital role of open dialogue in successfully navigating complex relationship dynamics, from setting boundaries to managing expectations and resolving conflicts.

Health and Safety Considerations

Different relationship models may have different health implications, particularly when it comes to sexual health. This section discusses how to navigate these challenges responsibly.

The Future of Relationships: What Lies Ahead?

As society becomes increasingly open to diverse forms of relationships, what does the future hold? Will alternative relationship models gain greater acceptance, or will monogamy continue to dominate? This section speculates on the likely trends and evolving attitudes.

Relationships, like sexuality itself, are complex and multifaceted, requiring a flexible, informed approach. By expanding our understanding of what relationships can be, we make room for richer, more diverse experiences that allow for genuine individual expression. This expanded perspective is both a product and a necessity of Sexual Revolution 2.0, representing yet another way in which our evolving views on sexuality promise to enrich our lives.

Chapter 12: Sex Work in the 21st Century

In the context of Sexual Revolution 2.0, the discussion around sex work is evolving at a rapid pace. Long considered a taboo and marginal sector, sex work is now gaining new dimensions of understanding and recognition. This chapter aims to provide a comprehensive overview of the current state of sex work, encompassing its legal, ethical, and social facets, and offering a glimpse into its future within an increasingly digitized and tolerant society.

Historical Context: The Stigma of Sex Work

Sex work has historically been shrouded in moral, legal, and ethical controversy. To fully understand the present and future landscape, it's essential to examine the origins of its associated stigmas and how these have permeated society over the years.

Definitions and Spectrum: Not Just Prostitution

Sex work encompasses a wide range of occupations, not just prostitution. From exotic dancing to webcamming, phone sex operations, and adult film participation, it is a varied industry with various facets that should not be lumped into a single category.

Ethical Concerns: Autonomy, Exploitation, and Consent

The ethics surrounding sex work have long been debated. While critics argue that it is inherently exploitative, a growing consensus contends that ethical sex work is possible and real, grounded in principles of autonomy, consent, and mutual respect.

Legal Perspectives: From Criminalization to Decriminalization

The legal treatment of sex work varies greatly worldwide, from full criminalization to limited forms of legalization and decriminalization. This section outlines the various approaches and their impacts on the safety, dignity, and rights of sex workers.

Feminist Views: Empowerment versus Oppression

Within feminist circles, sex work has been a topic of intense debate. While some see it as an empowering choice that allows for agency and autonomy, others view it as inherently oppressive. This section explores the nuanced arguments from both sides.

Technology and Its Role: The Digital Frontier

The internet has revolutionized many industries, and sex work is no exception. The digitization of services provides new opportunities and challenges, from camming and online platforms to digital currencies that promise anonymity but also add layers of complexity.

Sex Work and Public Health

Public health considerations are paramount in discussions around sex work. This section explores topics such as sexually transmitted infections, mental health, and the role of healthcare services tailored specifically for sex workers.

The Social Dynamics: Identity and Intersectionality

Sex work is intricately linked with questions of gender, race, and social class, and this intersectionality impacts how sex work is perceived and experienced. This section delves into these complex social dynamics.

Activism and Advocacy: Voices for Change

Sex workers themselves are increasingly at the forefront of advocacy and activism, fighting for recognition, rights, and safety. The chapter looks at some key organizations and movements driving change in this space.

The Future of Sex Work: An Evolving Landscape

With societal attitudes and norms around sexuality continually evolving, what does the future hold for sex work? This section speculates on upcoming trends, such as the normalization of various forms of sex work, advances in technology like AI and VR, and the potential for new legislative approaches.

Sex work in the 21st century is a complex and multi-dimensional issue that calls for a nuanced understanding and approach. The subject is central to Sexual Revolution 2.0, embodying many of the shifts in perception, legality, and technology that are reshaping our views on human sexuality. With ongoing advocacy and a fresh perspective, the once-marginalized sector is gradually gaining the recognition and regulation it deserves, thereby becoming an integral part of the broader conversation on sexual rights and freedoms.

Chapter 13: Law and Policy: Keeping Pace with Change

As the sexual landscape undergoes transformation in the era of Sexual Revolution 2.0, it becomes critical to evaluate how law and public policy are adapting—or failing to adapt—to these changes. Whether dealing with consent, sexual orientation, gender identification, or the very definition of what constitutes a sexual act, legislation often lags behind societal attitudes and scientific understanding. This chapter focuses on the intricate relationship between sexual progress and legal frameworks, highlighting the challenges and opportunities presented by the ever-changing landscape.

Legal Lag: When Law Can't Keep Up

Societal changes often outpace the ability of laws and policies to adapt, resulting in a discrepancy between what is socially accepted and what is legally permitted. This section outlines some key examples where laws have been slow to respond to societal shifts in attitudes about sex and relationships.

Consent Laws: The Evolution of "Yes Means Yes"

The concept of consent is now more nuanced than ever, particularly in a world increasingly dominated by digital interaction. This section discusses how legal frameworks around consent are evolving to be more explicit and affirmative, going beyond the simplistic "no means no."

Sexual Orientation and Gender Identity: Legal Recognition and Challenges

While significant strides have been made in the legal recognition of various sexual orientations and gender identities, challenges persist. Discrimination laws, hate crimes statutes, and policies around identification documents are discussed in this section.

Sex Work Legislation: A Global Perspective

Building on Chapter 12, this section delves into the complexities of sex work regulation on an international scale. Different countries offer different models for how to manage and regulate sex work, providing instructive examples for future policy-making.

Age and Sexual Activity: The Debate over Age of Consent

The legal age of consent varies dramatically around the world and even within countries. This section looks at the rationale behind these laws, the controversies they stir up, and the emerging trends that may influence future legislation.

Obscenity, Pornography, and Censorship

Laws around obscenity and pornography often reflect societal taboos more than rational policy. This section explores how these laws are changing in the face of new technology and more liberal social attitudes.

Reproductive Rights: An Ongoing Struggle

From abortion laws to access to contraceptives, reproductive rights are a critical part of the sexual landscape. This section examines how these rights are faring in legal terms and what challenges remain.

Data Privacy and Sexual Information

With the increasing digitization of our lives, data privacy becomes a concern in the realm of sexuality. This section discusses legal perspectives on the protection of sexual information, including revenge porn laws and the right to be forgotten.

Education Policies: What Are We Teaching the Next Generation?

Sex education is often the first formal encounter individuals have with sexual information, yet its regulation varies widely. This section examines the battles over sex education curricula and their implications for sexual health and well-being.

The Road Ahead: Legislative Predictions and Recommendations

Based on current trends, what can we predict for the future of sexual law and policy? This concluding section provides some speculative insights and recommendations for aligning law more closely with the lived realities and complexities of human sexuality.

Law and policy are fundamental frameworks that shape how society views and manages sexuality. They can either restrict or enable, stigmatize or normalize. It is crucial for these legal structures to evolve in tandem with societal changes to better serve the public's interests and safeguard individual freedoms. As we progress further into the era of Sexual Revolution 2.0, the law must not only reflect but also facilitate this evolution, opening up new horizons for how we understand, express, and regulate human sexuality.

Chapter 14: The Body Politic: Health, Wellness, and Sexuality

In the context of Sexual Revolution 2.0, the intersection of health, wellness, and sexuality takes on new dimensions of urgency and importance. Traditionally, conversations around sexual health have often been limited to the prevention of disease and unwanted pregnancies. However, in a rapidly evolving landscape where our understanding of sexuality is more nuanced than ever, it is crucial to expand this conversation to include mental health, emotional well-being, and even the social determinants that affect sexual health. This chapter examines the multifaceted ways in which health and wellness are inextricably linked with sexuality, and explores how public policy, medical research, and social attitudes influence these complex relationships.

Sexual Health: Beyond Disease and Pregnancy Prevention

While disease and pregnancy prevention are critical components of sexual health, a broader perspective also incorporates elements like sexual satisfaction, emotional well-being, and overall quality of life. This section offers an expanded definition of what constitutes sexual health in today's world.

Mental Health and Sexuality: A Symbiotic Relationship

The connection between mental health and sexuality is more profound than commonly acknowledged. Anxiety, depression, and other mental health conditions can profoundly affect sexual wellness, just as sexual difficulties can exacerbate mental health issues. This section delves into the symbiotic relationship between the two, backed by contemporary research.

Hormones, Medicine, and Sexuality

From birth control to hormone replacement therapy, pharmaceuticals have a profound impact on our sexual experiences and identities. This section examines how medicine both liberates and limits us, and how pharmaceutical companies and healthcare systems play a role in shaping sexual norms.

The Social Determinants of Sexual Health

Factors such as race, class, and education have a significant influence on sexual health outcomes. This section explores these social determinants and how they create disparities in access to sexual healthcare, information, and even in the quality of sexual experiences.

Navigating Healthcare Systems

From confidentiality concerns to finding LGBTQ+ friendly services, navigating the healthcare system can be a daunting task. This section offers practical advice and resources for receiving competent, compassionate sexual healthcare.

Wellness Practices and Sexuality

An emerging trend links wellness practices like mindfulness, yoga, and natural remedies to enhanced sexual experiences and well-being. This section scrutinizes the scientific evidence behind these claims and offers a balanced perspective.

Body Politics: Fat-shaming, Beauty Standards, and Sexuality

Body image significantly impacts sexual well-being, and social standards around beauty can become a form of oppression. This section tackles the politics of body image and how it intersects with sexuality, from fat-shaming to the celebration of different body types.

Sexual Trauma and Healing

Unfortunately, sexual trauma remains a pervasive issue affecting individuals across all demographics. This section focuses on the path to healing and how survivors can reclaim their sexual and overall well-being, emphasizing the importance of trauma-informed care.

Aging and Sexuality

Our sexual selves don't retire as we age, yet older adults often face unique challenges and stereotypes about their sexual health. This section breaks down the myths and explores the reality of sexuality in older age.

The Future: Where Do We Go From Here?

Drawing upon the key themes of this chapter, this section speculates on the future of health, wellness, and sexuality. What are the emerging trends, challenges, and opportunities? How can public policy and healthcare systems better adapt to the needs and realities of diverse sexual experiences?

Understanding the myriad ways in which health and wellness intersect with sexuality is integral to navigating the complexities of human experience. As society continues to advance in the era of Sexual Revolution 2.0, it becomes increasingly important to integrate a more holistic, inclusive perspective on sexual health and well-being. This chapter serves as both an examination of the present state and an aspirational roadmap for the future, urging policy makers, healthcare providers, and individuals alike to broaden their understanding and approach towards sexual health.

Chapter 15: The Future of Sexual Revolution: Ethical and Philosophical Considerations

As we stand on the cusp of a new era in human sexuality, it is imperative that we pause to consider the ethical and philosophical implications of Sexual Revolution 2.0. While technology, societal attitudes, and cultural shifts are rapidly changing the way we understand and engage with sexuality, it is crucial to navigate these transformations responsibly. This chapter delves into the various ethical conundrums and philosophical questions that arise as we move forward into uncharted territories of sexual expression and understanding.

The Ethics of Consent: Beyond Yes and No

Consent is at the core of ethical sexual interactions, but as we've seen in earlier chapters, the nuances are complex. In the age of digital encounters and increasingly diverse relationships, how do we ethically navigate consent in all its complexity?

The Morality of Pleasure

For centuries, various cultures and religions have placed moral judgments on sexual pleasure. As we forge ahead into a new era, how should we redefine or reconsider the moral dimensions of sexual pleasure and gratification?

The Social Contract: Collective Responsibilities

Sexuality is not solely an individual pursuit but also a collective social phenomenon. What responsibilities do we have to each other as members of a society undergoing a sexual revolution? This includes questions of public health, education, and general societal well-being.

The Virtual Realm: Avatars, AI, and Ethics

Technological advancements are blurring the lines between reality and virtuality in sexual experiences. What ethical considerations arise when our sexual partners are not just human but also digital or artificial entities?

Data Ethics and Privacy

As our sexual lives become increasingly digitized, ethical concerns about data collection, surveillance, and privacy are growing. How do we ethically manage and protect our most intimate data?

Exploitation and Equity

Sexual Revolution 2.0 holds the promise of liberation but also risks perpetuating exploitation and inequality. How do we ensure that advancements benefit a broad cross-section of society, rather than deepening existing inequities?

Reproductive Ethics: Designer Babies and Beyond

With CRISPR and other advancements in reproductive technology, we are entering a realm where choosing specific traits for offspring could become a reality. What are the ethical ramifications of these possibilities?

Environmental Considerations

From contraceptives to sex toys, the sexual revolution has a material footprint. What are the ethical responsibilities for sustainability in the production and consumption of products related to sexual health and pleasure?

Philosophical Foundations: A New Paradigm

As we redefine sexual norms, what philosophical theories best serve as a foundation for ethical sexual interaction? This section explores various philosophical frameworks from existentialism to utilitarianism and their applicability to the new sexual landscape.

The Future: Ethics in the Unknown

As we look towards an uncertain future, how do we prepare for ethical dilemmas that we can't yet foresee? What principles can guide us as we navigate unknown waters?

In the final analysis, every revolution comes with its set of ethical challenges and moral questions. Sexual Revolution 2.0 is no exception. As we break new ground in understanding and expressing human sexuality, ethical and philosophical considerations must be at the forefront of our collective consciousness. By engaging with these complexities, we can hope to foster a sexual landscape that is not only more liberated but also more responsible, equitable, and aligned with the highest ideals of human dignity and respect.

This concludes our exploration into the diverse and complex tapestry that is Sexual Revolution 2.0. Thank you for embarking on this intellectual journey, one that not only interrogates the present but also looks optimistically towards a future filled with both challenges and opportunities.